I'm Telling on You!

Brian Moses lives in Sussex with his wife and two daughters. He is actually an 'only child' but he sometimes invents brothers and sisters to inhabit the poems that he writes!

Lucy Maddison is a small illustrator who lives in Balham, London. She has three sisters all bigger than her, and much more bossy. Or so she says.

Also by Brian Moses and published by Macmillan

THE SECRET LIVES OF TEACHERS
Revealing Rhymes

MORE SECRET LIVES OF TEACHERS
More Revealing Rhymes

PARENT-FREE ZONE
Poems about parents and other problems

SCHOOL TRIPS

WE THREE KINGS
Christmas Poems

ALIENS STOLE MY UNDERPANTS
and other Intergalactic Poems

DON'T LOOK AT ME IN THAT TONE OF VOICE

I'm Telling on You!

poems about

brothers and sisters

Chosen by

Brian Moses

Illustrated by

Lucy Maddison

MACMILLAN CHILDREN'S BOOKS

For Poppy, Daisy and Teddy

First published 1999 by Macmillan Children's Books
This edition produced 2001 for
The Book People Ltd,
Hall Wood Avenue,
Haydock, St Helens WA11 9UL

ISBN 0 330 36867 2

3 5 7 9 8 6 4

A CIP catalogue record for this book is available from the British Library.

Printed by Mackays of Chatham plc, Chatham, Kent.

Contents

My Baby Brother's Secrets

When my baby brother
wants to tell me a secret,
he comes right up close.
But instead of putting his lips
against my ear,
he presses his ear
tightly against my ear.
Then, he whispers so softly
that I can't hear
a word he is saying.

My baby brother's secrets
are safe with me.

John Foster

Brother

B ehaves like a maniac when grown-ups aren't watching

R ampages most when you want to be quiet!

O rders you around as if you were his servant

T hinks endlessly of fresh ways to torment you

H ates above everything to hear you admired

E ats with loud noises simply to irritate

R esorts to being charming only as the last desperate bribe!

Brian Merrick

Sister

S weet as syrup whenever it suits her
our as old milk at all other times.

I s only good for messing things up, and
nterfering where she's absolutely no business.

S hows no brains, wit, or humour but always
impers like a moron when there's something she needs.

T eases and torments whenever you
ry to concentrate.

E xasperates all of your friends with her
xcruciating charm and smarminess.

R educes anyone with sense to rage and frustration and is
idiculously over-rated by everyone but me!

Brian Merrick

Where Are They?

'You've got your brother's hair!'
Said Auntie Claire.

'You've got your sister's nose!'
Said Auntie Rose.

I shook my head.

'Not me,' I said.
'I haven't touched them –
Honest!'

Trevor Harvey

I Like Insects

There's some that creep
Some that crawl
But the ones I like the best
Are the icky-sticky prickly ones
I shove down my brother's vest.

There's some that fly
Some that buzz
Some that wriggle in the dirt
I like to catch the hairy ones
And drop them down his shirt.

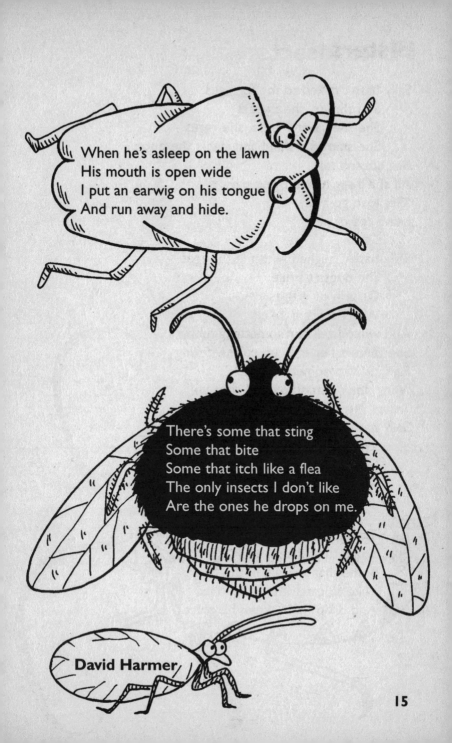

When he's asleep on the lawn
His mouth is open wide
I put an earwig on his tongue
And run away and hide.

There's some that sting
Some that bite
Some that itch like a flea
The only insects I don't like
Are the ones he drops on me.

David Harmer

Sisters

Sally hasn't talked to me for ages.
    She shouts, she swears
    She sneers and jeers, she rages
    She stamps around and slams the door
But doesn't *talk*.
All she'll say to me these days is
'Get lost, go away,
Leave me *alone!*'

Sally hasn't laughed with me for ages.
    She doesn't smile
    Or grin or giggle,
    Won't share a joke.
And when I tell her something funny
She throws her eyes up to the ceiling
Says, as if to someone else:
'Why don't that stupid kid shut up!'

Sally hasn't played with me for ages.
    We used to get the doll's house out,
    Go skipping in the street, or
    To the playground in the park together.
But now, it's like it never happened,
She's trying to pretend
Even to me
She's never *played* with anything, not ever.

Sally hasn't wanted me for ages.
     She's getting too *grown-up*
     To be seen with me,
     She reckons.
But I can get my own back, don't you worry.
It's nearly bedtime and I've hidden
The teddy bear
She sleeps with every night.

(And in a little while we'll see
How grown-up my sister Sally
Really is . . .)

Mick Gowar

Invisible Man

Sometimes I pretend I'm the invisible man.
I breathe very quietly,
I tiptoe everywhere.
Even my words become invisible
So I can't speak to anyone – not even to answer back.

When I'm invisible some grown-ups think I'm rude
or weird
but being invisible means I can't explain.

My mum always knows when I'm invisible,
she'll look straight through me and say,
'Where's that boy disappeared to again?'
or
'Watch what you're doing everyone, I think the invisible man
                might be about.'

WHERE'S THAT
BOY GONE?

But not my little sister.
She pretends she has special vision
and keeps telling everyone where I am.

Or she keeps bumping into me
and saying
'Oh sorry invisible man I didn't see you there.'

I know it's not nice
but when she does that I wish she'd disappear!

Philip Waddell

The Rival Arrives

Tom, take the baby out of the fridge
And put the milk back in.
We know you are not used to him
And think he makes a din,
But I'm afraid he's here to stay
And he is rather cute,
So you'll have to stop insisting
He goes in the car-boot.
And please stop telling all your friends
We bought him in a sale,
Or that he's a free sample
We received in the mail.
He was *not* found in a trolley
At the local Mothercare,
And a family did not give him to us
Because they'd one to spare.

You should look on the bright side, Tom.
In just a year or two
You will have someone else to blame
For the wicked things you do.

Brian Patten

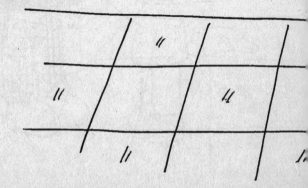

My Big Sister

No one's kissed her,
My big sister;
It's enough to make her weep.
Dreams of romance,
Thinks she's no chance,
So she cries herself to sleep.

She's tried make-up;
There's no take up,
No one ever looks her way.
Put her passion
Into fashion,
But the boys still stay away.

So, mum kissed her,
My big sister,
Said, 'You'll have to learn to wait.
You'll go steady,
When you're ready,
After all, you're only eight!'

Ray Mather

Cybersister

for Yvonne Johnstone

Oh, who'd have a sister like her?
A dog or a cat, I'd prefer.
She screams and she shouts,
with arms flailing about.
Oh, who'd have a sister like her?

A little bird whispered to me,
'Try connecting her to your PC.
Then transform her mind,
to a digital kind.'
A little bird whispered to me.

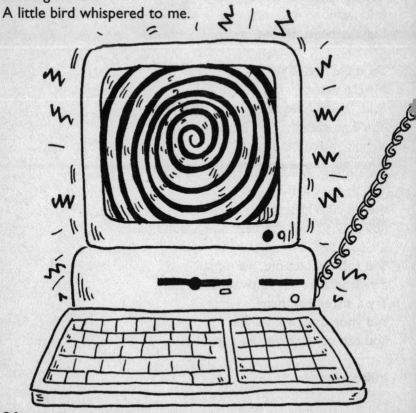

Now, my sister's the best one around!
She's polite and makes rarely a sound.
Yes, the finest thing yet —
she's a cute cyberpet,
now, my sister's the best one around.

You can contact me, via e-mail,
my 'Transister ™' software's for sale.
Try a sister, like mine,
and your days will be fine.
You can contact me, via e-mail.

Mike Johnson

Sisters

Tony Bradman

Please Yourself . . .

'Quick Mum, Billy's . . .'
'Now what have I told you about telling tales?'

'But Mum it's . . .'
'Sarah, I've told you once.'

'But Mum, if you don't . . .'
'Sarah – I won't tell you again!'

'Oh all right then – let the shed burn down . . .'

Clive Webster

Sometimes!

Sometimes he's a red Porsche 911,
Sometimes he's a fruit and nutcase from outer space,
Sometimes he's the lie that you wish was the truth
And sometimes he's . . . the warmth inside a smile.

Sometimes he's the flip and jump in a seaside wave,
Sometimes he's a packet of crisps when you have toothache,
Sometimes he's the itch in the sand between your toes
And sometimes he's . . . the twinkle in the black of a night sky.

Sometimes he's the exclamation mark in a sentence,
Sometimes he's a heavyweight boxing glove,
Sometimes he's a bag of multi-coloured crayons
And sometimes, and best of all, he's . . . simply my brother!

Ian Souter

Babies!

Babies are self-centred!
　　　　　bad-tempered!
I just can't see
　　　　　how anything
　　　　　　　　like THAT
　　　　　was ever, ever
　　　　　　　　ME!

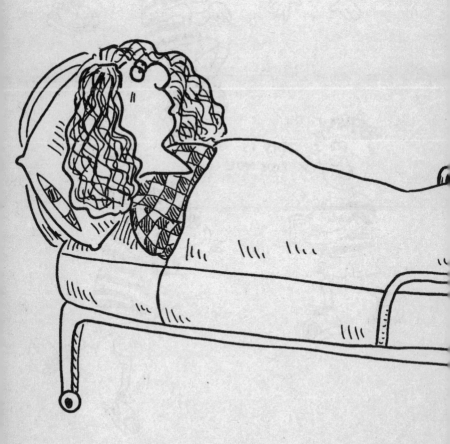

IT'S A BOY!

Asleep all the time
> or squawking,
no good at talking,
> except for ga-ga-ga
and goo-goo-goo!
> what good do they do?

Babies smell,
> babies yell!
I said to mum,
> I told her
babies should be born
> much older!

Matt Simpson

Own Backs

My brother is a dirty dog!
He whistles through his teeth,
Makes clacky noises when he eats
And gargles in his sleep!

He calls me *Horrible Hannah*
And sometimes *Smelly Feet!*
He deliberately untidies
The things that I keep neat,

Puts pepper in your cornflakes,
Salt in lemonade,
Mustard in your porridge,
Brown sauce in marmalade!

He'll never get to Heaven,
My brother Jim.
I don't think that Old Nick
Could even stomach him!

One day I'll get my own back
For all he's done and said:
I'll fill his room with black puddings
And nail a kipper under his bed!

Matt Simpson

Tests

If there were tests in complaining
then my brother would get full marks.
If there were tests in moaning and groaning
he'd be way out in front, no doubt.
If there were tests in arguing or fighting,
in getting his own way,
he'd win hands down any day.
If there were tests in being a pain,
in shouting or pouting,
in throwing a wobbly,
in tricking his mum or kicking his sister,
in fussing and feuding and falling out,
I know he'd be top of his class.
But give him a test in maths
and you'll only make yourself ill!
My brother's an ace at complaining
but his knowledge of figures is nil!

Brian Moses

The Bold Explorers

'Let's go on an Elephant Hunt!'
I shouted.
So off we ran,
Slashing at the ferns and the long grasses
With our brave sticks,
While Mum and Dad buttered our bread
And spread the cloth
At the edge of the wood.

After a while,
When we were tired of elephants
And our socks were full of seeds,
We threw down our frayed twigs,
Wiped our faces on grimy sleeves
And turned back.

The wood was different now.
The trees bunched tighter
Like thugs with greedy fingers,
And even the birds sang unkind tunes
To jangle our thoughts
Twist us in the wrong direction,
In all directions.

We met other families
With blank eyes and alien faces.
An old man shook his fists at us,
Said we frightened his chickens,
But we were the ones who ran . . .
Through the thorn bushes,
Over the ant heaps,
Past the hostile picnic people,
As far as a hot, tarmac road
Which lured us on and on.

It grew late,
Horribly late.
Our milky tea would be cold,
Our sandwiches curled.
Mum and Dad would have stopped worrying,
Started to growl and grumble instead.
There would be awful threats
And punishments that stretched to the end of time,
To the end of the long, black road.

When we heard our little dog barking
And saw the white cloth pulled tight as a frown
On the green moss
We did not cry because we had been lost.
We cried because we had been found.

Clare Bevan

A Sister Speaks

My brothers smell – in fact they stink.
Their thumbs are stained with purple ink.
They stick their tongues out, burp and wink,
And drop dead spiders in my drink.
If only I could make them shrink,
I'd sluice them down the kitchen sink.

Kate Williams

Listn Big Brodda Dread, Na!

My sista is younga than me.
My sista outsmart five-foot three.
My sista is own car repairer
And yu nah catch me doin judo with her.

    I sey I wohn get a complex.
    I wohn get a complex.
    Then I see the muscles my sista flex.

My sista is tops at disco dance.
My sista is well into self-reliance.
My sista plays guitar and drums
And wahn see her knock back double rums.

    I sey I wohn get a complex.
    I wohn get a complex.
    Then I see muscles my sista flex.

My sista doesn mind smears of grease and dirt.
My sista'll reduce yu with sheer muscle hurt.
My sista says no guy goin keep her phone-bound –
with own car mi sista is a wheel-hound.

    I sey I wohn get a complex.
    I wohn get a complex.
    Then I see muscles my sista flex.

James Berry

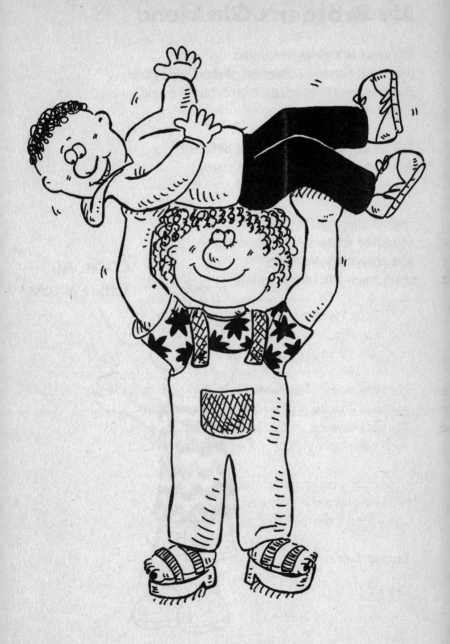

My Brother's Girlfriend

My brother's girlfriend thinks *I'm* weird!
I showed her my collection of dead woodlice
and the hairs from dad's beard, but she said,
'Ugh! You're disgusting.'

But what I say to her is, 'I'm different.'
Any kid can collect coins or stamps
but me I'd rather collect
ear wax,
toenail clippings,
squashed spiders
and chewed bubblegum
that's been left under tables.

LOOK AT THIS EARWAX!

And anyway, I don't think there's anything more weird than someone who *likes* snogging my big brother!

Brian Moses

My Little Sister

My little sister's got the loudest
scream in our school. She loves

SCREEEEEEEEEEAMING!

When she falls over in the playground
and hurts herself you can hear her

SCREEEEEEEEEEAMING!

five whole streets away. No one
except me can get her to stop

SCREEEEEEEEEEAMING!

46

once she's started. My Dad says it
sounds like a riot. So while she's

SCREEEEEEEEEAMING!

a teacher comes to fetch me
and I have to try and stop her

SCREEEEEEEEEEAMING!

I love my little sister but
I just wish sometimes she was more

quiet . . .

Tony Bradman

Big Sister . . .

Big sister,
what's this swelling on my face
do you suppose?

Don't worry, little brother.
That's a thing we call a NOSE.

Big sister,
there's this funny lump half up my leg.
You see?

Oh brother, don't be so alarmed.
That's what we call a KNEE.

Big sister,
this thing on my arm
I've had since I was small.

No need to worry, brother mine.
It's just a HAND, that's all.

But sister,
when the wind blows
I hear whistling and a hissing.

Oh brother,
that sounds really bad!
I think your brain is missing!

Barry Buckingham

Contrasts

My sister is fair weather
And I am foul.
I am stupid
And she's wise owl.

She is saint
And I am sinner.
She is dainty.
I pig my dinner.

I'm dull chalk.
She's fine cheese.
She's Father's darling.
I never please.

She's top of class.
I'm lowly dope.
She's faith and love,
And I'm no hope.

How can it be?
Same Father, Mother.

The real surprise?
We love each other!

John Kitching

The Dictator

My baby brother's red and cross
but, in our family, he's the boss.
Our mum obeys his every whim
and sits up half the night with him
and when he smiles, our mum and dad
are filled with joy. They must be mad.
His howls command, (that small dictator)
'Feed me NOW – right now, not later.'
Look! His mouth is stretched to bawl.
Do I love him? Not at all!

Marian Swinger

Race You

Race you back to the flat.
Race you up those steps.
Race you across that bridge.
Race you down the hill.
My brother and I
Are always having races.
He always wins
Because he's three years older
And much bigger and faster than me.
The only time I ever won
Was when he said:
'Race you across the pond.'
Half-way across he slipped.
He fell on the ice
And broke his wrist.

When I said I'd won,
He said, 'You only won
Because I slipped and fell.

That doesn't count.'
'Of course it does,' I said.
'Doesn't it, Mum?'
But she said,
'You and your races.
If you hadn't been racing,
This would never have happened.
It's all your fault.'

Why is it
That even when he loses,
My brother always wins?

He wouldn't even
Let me sign his plaster,
Until I said
It didn't count.

John Foster

Happy Families

My brother and I
get on quite well,
but it's not that we're under
some strange magic spell.

It's not even that
he's a special kind of brother,
it's simply because
we don't talk to each other!

Andrew Collett

My Little Sister

My little sister
doesn't kick, or thump, or scratch, or slog you,
my little sister
just wants to snog you . . .

And if you're not quick to escape
she'll nab you,
she'll take you by surprise
and grab you . . .

And it isn't a peck on the neck
or the briefest brush of the lips.

She's an artist who likes
to paint your face

with a sliding kiss
that seems like a snail
has left its trail on your cheek!

Brian Moses

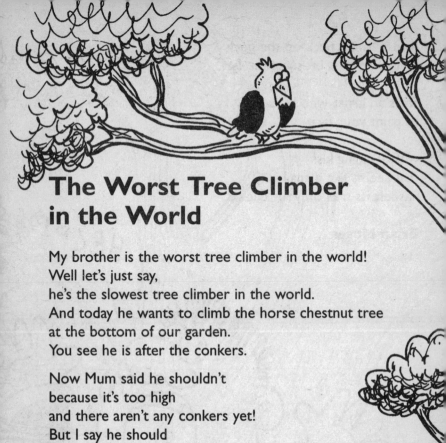

The Worst Tree Climber in the World

My brother is the worst tree climber in the world!
Well let's just say,
he's the slowest tree climber in the world.
And today he wants to climb the horse chestnut tree
at the bottom of our garden.
You see he is after the conkers.

Now Mum said he shouldn't
because it's too high
and there aren't any conkers yet!
But I say he should
because it's high
and there might be by the time he gets there!

Ian Souter

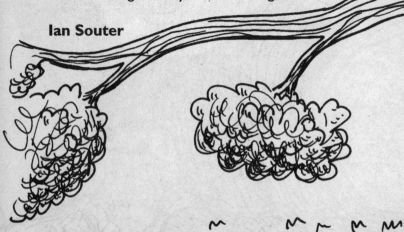

How to change your brother or sister for ever!!

Just copy/cut out and complete the form on the next page then get your brother or sister to sign it* and you are laughing!!!

* = Okay, this is the slightly difficult bit – getting him/her to actually sign. But try:

i) asking him/her to sign in the middle of the night when s/he is so tired that s/he doesn't have a clue what s/he is signing – or,
ii) smiling REALLY nicely at him/her

GOOD LUCK!!!!

James Carter

I, ... [his/her name] **promise:**

a) to be INCREDIBLY nice to .... [your name] until
   at least the year 2050

b) to ALWAYS give .... [your name] the free gift out
   of the breakfast cereal

c) to clean out the rabbit hutch/cat litter tray/leopard cage
   EVERY WEEK

d) to say 'Can I do ANYTHING for you?' whenever you see
   .... [your name]

e) to forget the phrase 'It wasn't me, it was
   .... [your name]' TOTALLY

f) to NEVER mention again what .... [your name] did in
   the bath as a baby

I also promise that if I fail to keep to this agreement (in any way
at all) I will have to pay £2 every week to .... [your name]
until s/he says so.

Signed ....

Date . . / . . / . .

PETER DIXON'S GRAND PRIX OF POETRY

A chicane of flying verse by the Formula One poet,
Peter Dixon, illustrated by David Thomas

Magic Cat

My mum whilst walking through the door spilt some
magic on the floor.
Blobs of this
and splots of that
but most of it upon the cat.
Our cat turned magic, straight away
and in the garden went to play
where it grew two massive wings
and flew around in fancy rings.
'Oh look!' cried Mother, pointing high, 'I didn't
know our cat could fly.'
Then with a dash of Tibby's tail
she turned my mum into a snail!
So now she lives beneath a stone
and dusts around a different home.
And I'm an ant
and Dad's a mouse
and Tibby's living in our house.

A selected list of poetry books available from Macmillan

The prices shown below are correct at the time of going to press. However, Macmillan Publishers reserve the right to show new retail prices on covers which may differ from those previously advertised.

The Secret Lives of Teachers   0 330 34265 7
    Revealing rhymes, chosen by Brian Moses   £3.50

'Ere We Go!   0 330 32986 3
    Football poems, chosen by David Orme   £2.99

Aliens Stole My Underpants   0 330 34995 3
    Intergalactic poems chosen by Brian Moses   £2.99

Revenge of the Man-Eating Gerbils   0 330 35487 6
    And other vile verses, chosen by David Orme   £2.99

Teachers' Pets   0 330 36868 0
    Chosen by Paul Cookson   £2.99

Parent-Free Zone   0 330 34554 0
    Poems about parents, chosen by Brian Moses   £2.99

I'm Telling On You   0 330 36867 2
    Poems chosen by Brian Moses   £2.99

All Macmillan titles can be ordered at your local bookshop or are available by post from:

Book Service by Post
PO Box 29, Douglas, Isle of Man IM99 1BQ

Credit cards accepted. For details:
Telephone: 01624 675137
Fax: 01624 670923
E-mail: bookshop@enterprise.net

Free postage and packing in the UK.
Overseas customers: add £1 per book (paperback)
and £3 per book (hardback).